THE FUTURE H

African
POETRY
BOOK SERIES

Series editor: Kwame Dawes

THE FUTURE HAS AN APPOINTMENT WITH THE DAWN

Tanella Boni

Translated by Todd Fredson
Introduction by Honorée Fanonne Jeffers

University of Nebraska Press / Lincoln and London

Acknowledgments for the use of copyrighted
material appear on page 71, which constitutes
an extension of the copyright page.

The African Poetry Book Series has been made
possible through the generosity of philanthropists
Laura and Robert F. X. Sillerman, whose
contributions have facilitated the establishment
and operation of the African Poetry Book Fund.

Library of Congress Cataloging-in-Publication Data
Names: Boni, S. Tanella, author. | Fredson,
Todd, translator. | Jeffers, Honorée Fanonne,
1967–writer of introduction.
Title: The future has an appointment with the
dawn / Tanella Boni; translated by Todd Fredson;
introduction by Honorée Fanonne Jeffers.
Other titles: Avenir a un rendez-vous avec l'aube. English
Description: Lincoln: University of Nebraska
Press, 2018. | Series: African poetry book series
| Includes bibliographical references.
Identifiers: LCCN 2018006596
ISBN 9781496211859 (pbk.: alk. paper)
ISBN 9781496212849 (epub)
ISBN 9781496212856 (mobi)
ISBN 9781496212863 (pdf)
Subjects: LCSH: Côte d'Ivoire—Poetry.
Classification: LCC PQ3989.2.B6263 A9513
2018 | DDC 841/.914—dc23 LC record available
at https://lccn.loc.gov/2018006596

Set in Garamond Premier by E. Cuddy.

CONTENTS

Parce que je me dis que je prends cette langue
que je vais utiliser et puis,
je vais essayer peut-etre de la transformer, de dire en francais
ce que moi, J'ai envie de dire.

[Because I tell myself that I'll take this language
that I'm going to use and
perhaps I'll try to transform it, to say in French
what it is that I want to say.]
—Tanella Boni

This collection of verse, *The Future Has an Appointment with the Dawn* by Tanella Boni, is extraordinary, combining historical knowledge with skilled craft. But if it hadn't been translated from the French, you never would have read it, even though Boni is a renowned West African writer who has published widely. This is where we start, because any Western reader will ask *why* when offered the work of a non-Western writer.

Most American readers only consume literature published in English. This is especially true when it comes to African literature. African novelist and critic Ngũgĩ Wa Thiong'o has been averse to writing in the European colonizer's language, and this remains an appropriate concern. The emphasis on English shields the lives of non-Anglophone Africans from American readers, but the practical issue is that many American readers are not fluent in other languages. (I am not, though I took those required two years of foreign language back in college.)

Translation is important, but history and cultural connections are too. For example, the Black Arts Movement ended more than forty years ago, and we are more than eighty years past the Harlem Renaissance. Writers of both eras were prolific, producing work that traversed waters to connect with others of African descent around the globe, and in this twenty-first-century moment, we bear witness to a (re)new(ed) literary era that privileges the lives, history, and political possibilities of black people. Here we are again, despite some critics' premature arguments against "race writing."[1] It is an exciting time. However, although this current, racialized iteration resembles similar eras, for many in the United States, *black* poetry now means only *North American* poetry, and it does not refer to the rich, global diaspora of poets of African descent.

Consider French African writers. Few American readers are familiar with the Martiniquais Aimé Césaire, who coined the term "Negritude" to apply to African literature overtly concerned with African lives, or with the Senegalese Léopold Senghor, who dusted off "francophone," an archaic term, and repurposed it to apply to literature of French Africa. Along with Léon Damas, Césaire and Senghor are known as the *trois pères*—the three fathers—of the Negritude movement, which began in the thirties. Yet as unfamiliar as many American readers are with these men, even fewer know of Paulette and Jane Nardal, the Caribbean sisters who introduced African American writers to French African writers in Paris.[2]

Even black readers in America mostly consume books in English, including when they read African literature, and most of the literature by Africans published (or made available) in the United States was originally written in English. One must be curious indeed to find African female writers translated from French to English, and even more so to find these writers' translated poetry—that eternal literary stepchild.

This is precisely why the work of Tanella Boni is so important. Her publication record is substantial, and she is critically acclaimed as well.

Those qualifications represent obvious reasons for picking up this book. And I've argued that in this twenty-first-century black literary moment, a reconnection with African writers is needed, and not only those who write in English. As many American readers, black or otherwise, face the meaning of history, considering its impact on black people globally, Boni's work offers monumental concerns.

A richer understanding of Boni's verse arises with some background context, and fortunately her translator, Todd Fredson, has done a superlative job (along with presenting her poetry in English). His "Translator's Note" (included in this volume) gives an overview of contemporary history of Côte d'Ivoire and, in particular, the political corruption or discord in that country. Like earlier Negritude and Francophone poets, Boni is concerned with the Pan-African impulse, as evidenced by her poetry collection on Gorée Island. Although located in Senegal and not Côte d'Ivoire, Gorée continues to occupy metaphorical space for black folks, both in Africa and elsewhere. It is the ancestral site of a major slave-trading fort, through which many thousands—perhaps as many as a million—Africans passed, on their horrific journey on the Middle Passage into slavery. Another one of her books, *There are no happy words* (*Il n'y a pas de parole heureuse*), addresses the Rwandan genocide.

In this translated collection, Boni continues to distill history, and there are two ways to approach this book. One reader may prefer to follow the poet's verse without accompanying information; only after completing the collection will that reader go back and read the notes. Another reader might decide to examine Fredson's "Translator's Note," continue to Boni's notes, and only then enter the poems, searching out specific, historical allusions. I read Boni's collection several times and can testify that both approaches proved equally satisfying. First, I read the book without the notes: I wanted to experience the language before anything else.

The poems are grouped into brief sections, and no poem has a title. Within each section are several meditative, economical units. These units are self-contained, and yet, there's a story being told. Each unit connects to the preceding and subsequent unit, and each one carries sacred weight. This ephemeral device articulates the wisdom of proverb, with timeless images peppered by contemporary suggestions. Unidentified first- and second-person pronouns—*We, our,* and *you*—allow any reader of any nationality to identify with this place and its inhabitants.

At the beginning of the collection, an "Eden" appears, along with sacred ancestors who work and live off the land, happy in their innocence. The allusion is obvious, recalling creation myths of the Bible and the Qu'ran. (Both Christianity and Islam are dominant religions in Côte d'Ivoire.) The phrase "ribs of the aurora" evokes divine and corporeal foundations, the sky where the Abrahamic God resides, and the earth from which this God formed humanity, though here, Adam's body is reduced to merely a means for Eve's creation.

In later verse units, this Eden is violated and these first inhabitants lose their innocence. They hear "the speech of the hyena," that animal of misfortune, and the innocents are violated and perhaps killed: "our daily lives placed among the objects for sale / at the market rapacious for our distressed skins." An unidentified human tyrant violates this ancient people's unified understanding: "You construct the puzzle / of the city model you say / on the unknown sand of the ancestors." These lines allude to the building of a structure reaching to the heavens, and once again, Boni might be addressing the Tower of Babel in the Bible, while the Qu'ran mentions a similar tower. Though in each story, both structures are built by separate rulers, each man's arrogance leads to his downfall and sown discord among his subjects.

However, if we apply the historical information contained in the notes, the earlier-mentioned Eden might refer to a knowable locale, West African forests, formerly dense but now in danger of deforestation. Thus, this ancestral innocence would occur in the precolonial era, the time before slavery became a major economic foundation of West African economy. The violation of ancestors and their homes would refer to that trade, a practice that continues to concern Boni: "our daily lives placed among the objects for sale / at the market rapacious for our distressed skins / our history dreams of erasing these poverty lines." Certainly, we wouldn't be visiting a territory that carries the name Côte d'Ivoire, for we would occupy a time before the Berlin Conference of 1884–85, and the resulting Scramble for Africa, when the continent was divided among European colonists and the French took the lion's share of territory.

Other poems in the collection veer away from Africa. We enter the deposing of Charles X of France, the attack of Grecians by Ottomans, the use of Guernica as a Nazi bombing site. Yet though these poems address non-African locales and events, there is no disruption. Each place Boni encounters has its own innocence, and the speaker narrates with clear-eyed witness and restrained grief. The *we* and *you* still occupy these lines, and Boni's tonal consistency is impressive. The penultimate poem in the collection references the connections between these seemingly disparate places, territories to which she has not traveled in real life. But Boni is a moral navigator, challenged by her task: "How to speak the beauty of the world / when life's hope / crumbles like yarrow."

NOTES

Epigraph: Nicki Hitchcott, *Women Writers in Francophone Africa* (Oxford: Berg, 2000), 4.

1. I refer to Kenneth Warren's *What Was African American Literature* (Cambridge MA: Harvard, 2012).

2. Jennifer Anne Boitin, "In Black and White: Gender, Race Relations, and the Nardal Sisters in Interwar Paris," *French Colonial History* 6, no. 1 (January 2005): 119–35.

TRANSLATOR'S NOTE

Todd Fredson

In her first two collections, *Labyrinthe* (*Labyrinth*) in 1984 and *Grains de sable* (*Grains of sand*) in 1993, Ivorian poet Tanella Boni expressed a certain optimism, or, as critic Marie-Clémence Adom elaborates: the poems remember "the sweetness of a life which, if it does not embody total happiness, looks a lot like it."[1] But Boni's third collection, *Il n'y a pas de parole heureuse* (*There are no happy words*), published in 1997, broke dramatically with that optimism. The sweetness of hope gave way to "an extreme skepticism" verging on nihilism (Adom). This shift was perhaps unavoidable given that the Rwandan genocide had occurred between these collections. The 1994 genocide is a point of reflection in *There are no happy words*. In it, Boni struggles to trust language. What language, after all, could adequately register such atrocity? The words themselves become "pools of forgetting."

The Rwandan genocide was the most visible and extreme reaction to the legacy of European colonialism and the continued efforts of G7 nations to apportion African resources—the most visible reaction, anyway, for the non-African international community. The Rwandan horror was not, of course, the only wrenching dissolution taking place. Following the end of the Cold War, a "wave of democracy" spread across Africa. In practical terms, what this meant was that the United States and its allies no longer needed to support leaders who served as bulwarks against African socialism. Without the imposition of global ideologies, fighting over resources often heightened existing ethnic tensions and gave rise to extreme nationalism. As autocrat Joseph Mobutu in the Democratic Republic of the Congo lost Western support, the wars that followed produced what is often called Africa's World War. The nineties in sub-Saharan Africa also saw civil wars in Burundi, Sierra Leone, Liberia, and Guinea-Bissau and the Tuareg rebellion in Mali and Niger. The wave of democracy was also a wave of civil wars. In the Ivory Coast the nineties were also a period of destabilization that saw a rise in ethnic conflict. The Ivory Coast had been, for its perceived stability and facile integration into the world market following independence in 1960, "nicknamed Miracle," as Boni writes here in *L'avenir a un rendez-vous avec l'aube* (*The future has an appointment with the dawn*). But for the country nicknamed Miracle, the millennium concluded with a military coup on Christmas Eve. This Christmas surprise

> flaunted its wings
> under the windows
> in the city streets
> before the huts
> across the open countryside.

A response to rampant government corruption, the coup seemed, for a moment, like an opportunity. Ivorian leaders had profited as they drove the Ivory Coast into ineradicable debt and, simultaneously, eliminated public services, communal land rights, and educational access. These policies were driven by international lenders, namely the World Bank and the International Monetary Fund (IMF), whose loan conditions were meant to establish land tenure laws and labor conditions that were favorable to foreign investors. Perhaps the coup was, as political anthropologist Mike McGovern suggests, a signal to Ivorian elites that the "lifestyles to which they had been accustomed while distributing the patronage that had been the basis" of political legitimacy had reached a generational terminus.[2] Perhaps the shake-up could move the Ivory Coast away from its lopsided relationship with former colonizer France. One leading presidential candidate for the 2000 election, Laurent Gbagbo, promised a second independence movement. Gbagbo proposed a structural change in order to enact a truer sovereignty. In practice, however, this proposal took a radically nativist turn.

A constitutional revision of eligibility for presidential candidates eliminated Gbagbo's most significant competition, and Gbagbo won the disputed 2000 election. He capitalized on ethno-cultural resentments that largely originated during the post-independence boom and which had been kindled by the increased competition for the country's restricted resources and services. The first president of the Ivory Coast, Félix Houphouët-Boigny, who ruled from 1960 until his death in 1993, had ignored ethnically defined territorial claims as he promoted national agricultural development. The country's economic success early on obscured many of the sociocultural frictions. Any dissidence was also quietly, but harshly, suppressed. Gbagbo himself was jailed twice. As faculty at the country's largest university, Gbagbo was jailed from 1971 to 1973 for subversive teaching and in 1992 for organizing student protests. Many intellectuals supported Gbagbo's aspiration to push out the foreign influence that Houphouët-Boigny and his successor, Henri Bedié, had invited in. Gbagbo, however, aiming to broaden his appeal, expanded his definition of foreigner. It included not only those representing Western interests, but Ivorians whose ethnic affiliations did not entitle them to autochthonous land claims, particularly in the fertile south. This, in effect, would evict Ivorians whose affiliations were with the country's northern ethnic groups, most of which share kinship with groups in neighboring Mali and Burkina Faso.

Gbagbo's choice to exploit the ethno-cultural resentments disappointed many of his former colleagues. Boni was a colleague of Gbagbo's at the university and has known his wife, Simone, since they attended *lycée* together in their teens. Boni reflected in one of our conversations: "After he got to power—you just don't know what a person is thinking." Ethnic violence erupted around the presidential election, and then the country fell into a north-south civil war that lasted from 2002 to 2007.

Boni removed herself to the Île de Gorée just off the coast of Dakar, Senegal, in the immediate aftermath of the election. On the Île de Gorée, Boni wrote within view of the House of Slaves, a memorial to the Africans shipped as slaves to the Americas. Meditating on its Door of No-return, Boni wrote a collection titled *Gorée île baobab* (*Gorée island baobab*); the baobab is the African tree often used as an image to symbolically (romantically, reductively) portray sub-Saharan Africa. Reflecting on the significance of the memorial, the coming and going of tourists, children playing on the island, and the events in her life, she looks across the water to America, as it sends its military to Iraq. "Bagdad the beautiful murdered," she writes, "[t]he cliffs of reason collapse / [t]here is no more tended hedge to stifle / [t]he madness that fans the world."

She published her fourth collection, *Chaque jour l'espérance* (*Each day, hope*), in 2002 and her fifth collection, *Ma peau est fenêtre d'avenir* (*My skin is a window looking onto the future*), in 2004. *Gorée island baobab* was also published in 2004. Her novel *Matins de couvre-feu* (*Mornings after curfew*) came out in 2004 too, as the civil war in the Ivory Coast saturated daily life. Boni's novel gained attention, making her a target of police surveillance and of hostility from increasingly violent student groups. Boni self-exiled to France, which was the only border that remained open to her, she explains—her husband, an economist, had departed earlier for a post in Burkina Faso. "I left," she told me, "like a refugee, holding one valise."

Mornings after curfew received the Ahmadou Kourouma Prize in 2005. In 2009 Boni won the Antonio Viccaro International Poetry Prize, awarded by the United Nations Educational, Scientific, and Cultural Organization (UNESCO) for her body of work. Boni had, long before, started this book, her seventh collection. She worked on *The future has an appointment with the dawn* for ten years. It was published in 2011, as the French and UN intervened to forcibly end the second Ivorian civil war, which was sparked by the 2010 presidential election, the first since Gbagbo's controversial win in 2000. French and UN military forces bombed the presidential palace to remove Gbagbo, who refused to concede in what appeared to be a narrow loss. The international community recognized Alassane Ouattara as the new president. Ouattara is considered the northern candidate—the one for whom the constitutional revisions in 2000 were most intended to prohibit from running. A U.S.-educated economist, Ouattara is a former deputy managing director at the IMF. Boni tentatively returned to the Ivory Coast in 2013.

The future has an appointment with the dawn confirms Boni's desire to hope against the seemingly inevitable returns of ethno-cultural violence and state brutality. Desiring to hope and hoping itself, though, should not be conflated. The first section of the book, "Land of Hope," chronicles the cohabitation of inhabitants marked by difference, as well as those "adrift and without origin." As the peace in that edenic space ruptures, politicians, who increasingly deplete the meaning of language with their promises and explanations, make assurances that they will control the forces at work, as if they could control the wind. Section two of the book, "A murdered life," recounts the killing of a young man during ethnic and political violence in the Ivory Coast in 2000. As Boni concludes, she ties her consideration to paintings by Eugène Delacroix, *Liberty Leading the People* and *The Massacre at Chios*, as well as *Guernica* by Pablo Picasso, in order to include the Ivorian violence in a lineage of ethno-cultural irruptions that extend beyond the African continent.

The future has an appointment with the dawn maps the events in the Ivory Coast onto a mythic topography. Humans participate in an existential, if not quite universal, drama. They are there among ancestors, and subject to the whims of the powerful, who are at once magical and all too petty. The elements—the sun, the wind, the water—are animated beyond mere simile or metaphor; they are independent forces. The word, too, is elemental, and the poet is present in the landscape—"during these times / I searched for the letters / for the perfect word." She is committed to the enigma, even the folly, of language, as if the right phrase, like a spell or a curse, could restore meaning, could arrest the unraveling, the descent, the gravity that keeps pulling bodies into the earth. As Adom considers Boni's poetry, she notes that in African orature it is common practice for storytellers to establish the tone of a telling by introducing the account with riddles, or by distorting the medium of the presentation itself. It prepares the audience for elements of the fantastical. Here, in Boni's telling, the ethnic violence is beyond belief. But it is also too real to be assigned a purely symbolic value. The unbelievable tale is also a lived experience. Her myth is imbued with an individual pathos.

This is consistent with Boni's poetic style. Boni, according to critic Bruno Gnaoulé-Oupoh, is able to make crucial assessments of "man's ongoing quest for greater well-being" through her "distant, detached" but "remarkably lucid" point of view.[3] She is, at the same time, regularly credited with being among the writers—writers such as Syl Cheney-Coker, Véronique Tadjo, and Bernard Kojo Laing—who transitioned West African literature away from the literary realism of the late seventies and early eighties and into a highly subjective terrain.[4] Adom describes Boni's poetry, as it broke from predecessors, as reflecting "a psychological, personal, and intimate experience." Boni's perspective is both aerial and intimate. Reproducing this perspective in the translation has been my guiding objective.

The poetry, over the years it was written, developed toward a spare lyricism. In her search for "letters for the perfect word," the medium, language, is scrutinized. At the same time, though, the language must not become clouded by the scrutiny. The language-under-scrutiny must remain transparent—there is a tale being told, after all. This transparency is the key to her ability to be, simultaneously, precise and vast. Within the tale, for example, as actions are portrayed, there is a minute decision being made again and again by the author: the evocative image or the simple exact verb? Will an imagistic interpretation over-determine the reader's emotional engagement? Will the single exact verb preserve the reader's intellectual engagement?

While achieving that balance—the ideal viscosity of the medium, as it were—has been my guiding objective, it is secondary to understanding the cultural dynamics of the Ivorian conflict. No matter what facility I may have with the languages—in this case, French and English, and West African orature and poetry writing, more generally—there are just some feelings that I am unsure I could tease out of the language into English without access to the cultural experience at hand. And here I have been helped, I suppose, by having lived in the Ivory Coast directly following the Christmas coup, from early 2000 to mid-2002. The sociopolitical history that is woven into this collection, the violence taking shape, the forces unveiling themselves, donning their uniforms—this feeling of violence emerging is something I can never forget. Gaining conceptual understanding of a work is a matter of degrees, I suppose. I should say, simply, that I feel more able to translate *The future has an appointment with the dawn* into an American context having been grounded in the experience of the Ivorian conflict myself.

Let me add one final note on a specific translation decision that illustrates these two translation principles at work. Boni capitalizes the word "Amitié," elevating the character of the water with which it is associated. "The water's Friendship" or "water's Harmony" is an instance of the phrase in translation (and, later, "the deep river of," and "in the water of "). This abstraction in its water-form is a restorative element. I think "Harmony" would have been, semantically, sufficient as a translation. But I saw the opportunity to peer into the word itself if I instead chose "Kindness." I take it at its most literal, "of a kind," and recognize the "kin" that is at the heart of that word. In "Kindness" is the warmth and solidarity that haunts the political violence; it is the wellspring of such heartbreak, where kinship, or ethno-cultural identity, has been used to fracture Ivorian social relations. I hope to acknowledge Boni's deliberation over the balance of the medium, language, and the way it steers our vision, ideally compelling us to look inward, and at what is right here at our feet, while also allowing us to see or sense the eternal, in which we are operating, and to which we are obliged.

NOTES

1. Marie-Clémence Adom, "Autopsie des indépendances africaines; une lecture de Il n'y a pas de parole heureuse, de Tanella Boni," *Revue Baobab* 10 (January 14, 2013), https://www.revuebaobab.org/content/category/5/30/33/. This and translations throughout are mine.
2. Mike McGovern, "This Is Play: Popular Culture and Politics in Côte d'Ivoire," in *Hard Work, Hard Times: Global Volatility and African Subjectivities*, edited by Anne-Marie Makhulu, Beth A. Buggenhagen, and Stephen Jackson (Berkeley: University of California Press, 2010), 74.
3. Bruno Gnaoulé-Oupoh, *La littérature ivoirienne* (Abidjan: Karthala, 2000).
4. See Odile Cazenave and Patricia Célérier, *Contemporary Francophone African Writers and the Burden of Commitment* (Charlottesville: University of Virginia Press, 2011), 49; and Stephanie Newell, "Laing, B[ernard] Kojo (1946–)" in *Encyclopedia of Post-Colonial Literatures in English*, edited by Eugene Benson and L. W. Conolly (New York: Routledge, 2005), 794.

THE FUTURE HAS
AN APPOINTMENT
WITH THE DAWN

LAND OF HOPE

I

The dawn counted its nomadic steps
to the border
the early breeze took over
amid the day's news
the men and the women
weaved a unity cloth
with sympathetic hands

it was ordinary life
between routine and rupture
during these times
I searched for letters
for the perfect word

The land of hope was blessed by the gods
here and there words sang
the refrain of water's Kindness
the poet woke early that morning
not knowing how long
the offerings of this ground
would nourish those adrift and without origin

Sowings were good
the harvests miraculous
the poet lived
on a parcel of land in Eden's garden
breath she said
you are not of this world
naked-winged swallow
your feathers wait so long
for buoyant winds from the open sea
they will borrow the ribs
of the aurora
and rise to the roof of the world

II

Beyond my path
across this expanse of mountaintop
a song stronger more deafening
a martial cadence from nowhere
rhythm from the tank shelling the dead
another music ignoring the past
bursts of wind sweeping the future away
crack of dawn
an emergency C-section
breath from a country laboring under drip
generation rapidly deteriorating
the sun's difficult
birth into the high point of day
nowhere the right word
the poet must wed these visions
of the dying world
and the living water that keeps the hearts beating

We dream sparks stars moons and suns
lighting our lives our days sweeping clear the path
the time-to-be braids its palm branch canopy
I do not know how to tell you this story of the blood
that cuts our lives loose at the door of the wind
how to tell you that the coming dawn
has already changed the color of this motionless day
that the wait lacerates our grieving hearts
while infusions of cold hard cash
are blatantly burned throughout the night

III

Our conspicuous steps wake
the ancestors nodding off
in the unfamiliar shadow
that is out ahead of the morning sun

history still slumbers
in the bed of the first word of love
it will come to save us from open chaos
from our quicksand steps
we wait for the first blue love note with feverish hands
face offered to the wind to the sun
eyelids heavy with rain

the day has sown the word of the hyena
in the city the night
the speech of the hyena terrorizes words stripping them

Humans do you say we are
living in the land of wild beasts
beyond rivers and grottoes
forests and savannas
tomorrow the future has an appointment with the dawn
and no one yet imagines the traffickers for this route

Those architects of untouchable borders
and their odd-colored tracers
have opened the trails of the dead
their thousand-sense words
dip the soul of such political speech
into a box of riddles
that they have appointed
the well-of-newfound-meanings

who will still believe
that the spirit is upright and hard-working
that the educated reason
thinks and transforms
life into an island of happiness

And I look straight at the eyes of day
it is veil and silence
riveted to this land of origins
it doesn't say a word
enframed by the rainbow's shadow

you construct the puzzle
of the city model you say
on the unknown sand of the ancestors
already night falls in the daytime
and your smile exacts the difference
between the moonlight and the sunbeam

the offended sky tears at the seams
this night lays strands of hatred
across Hope's canvas

a silver bead weights the wing of time

Smile and hoard the time that is coming
the wind has a sense the whirlwind too
smile at the treasure
this time that keeps new life
from hazarding into the eye of the storm
but there is strength greater than the wind's
richer more powerful

the expected death
the tribute from each criminal hand
positioned to the left of the heart
faux-leftist values embedded
by way of your honeyed words
and your bloody sword

IV

Every morning
the hour of headlines resounds in the streets
before the rooster's first crow
hour that opens a path to the convulsing dawn
competing newspapers attire themselves in blue and red
the crowd drinks at the source of the poison
lapping at double-talk
and the blank words
flow through the veins of that day's gravediggers
rising blot by blot back up to the eyes
blurring the look of the world
squares rectangles circles and triangles

But every geometric figure is an illusion
intended to wake the transient butterflies
travelers beyond myths
and unprovable principles

We live among messiahs in a time of messages
litanies old and barbed
raised around the huts
huts closed within a frail smile of misery
our daily lives placed among the objects for sale
at the market rapacious for our distressed skins
our history dreams of erasing these poverty lines
and courtyards of cripples
dreams of making us happier

Happiness's shoreline is far
from the paths of our former glory
and tomorrow sleeps
its breathing too shallow
there at the sill of dreamland

the sea has lost the color of better days
forgotten the importance of a palette well-mixed
enough to bless the horizon sand to sky
I don't know how to count the raindrops anymore
immense heavy engraving the hours
behind this curtain of eternal dawning

V

The distance no longer separates heaven and earth
but walks backward among the humans
who sing oblivion ignoring forgiveness
the years catch up with the sun
when the living give up speech

still the horizon remembers
the country we inhabit

What potholed frontage
will open to a country with living people
what handshake
will trigger the hymn
of a unity that is woven out of more than bloodlines
the daytime air annihilates such a convergence
I imagine it born on the rainbow's clouds
free between sea and sun on the four winds

I dream the poem of a borderless sea
I dance a welcoming music in my skin
first ground for any home
while the hands of plenty the portly souls
weave their barbed wire
I don't know if we live together
at a crossroad of equal distribution

here forget the alchemy of dreams
the sense of an essential mixture

Look at the hues and contours of this land o you that depart
the name of each pilgrim moving
into the hard valley of life
is no longer etched on the mountaintop

those who love to smash the stone
have always gathered at dawn
in the roundabout of sorcerers
who dip their hands in the fire
because nobody refashions
the same principles a thousand times
without sacrificing the best of his soul
into a basket of provisional interests
handed around by those
who promise to hold the wind at bay

And the wind rises and time sculpts
a whirlwind that reveals that climbs
then descends the steps of the sand temple
as if the twelve labors of Hercules
once a point of fact
were just a bedtime story for people
after a hard day of hoping

VI

Yesterday we all swam together
in the deep river of Kindness
we were catfish and tilapia circling in
the salvific water of riverbeds
that have dried up over time

after the passage of thunder
scorched our dreams of the water

and the tree of relation's branches were splintered
to a thousand pieces

Look at these lineages
shreds falling
the people ripped into pieces
no longer recognize their own markings
at this time of the weaver's flight
into heaven's receding heights

one day they had all laughed together
birds at their migratory stop
around the source of their innumerable decorations
but time arranged its treasures haphazardly
each appointed his own
according to a name that controlled his tongue
each took root
fastening itself to that skin

Another day the words were flung wide into dust
tricked into ruts
they failed in the public square
the quarry of a single language
powder keg of one thousand accents
ready to explode at the slightest inflammatory whisper

VII

The migratory birds then
transformed into sedentary humans
today do they look at themselves
machete play
machine guns waving
clubs on their left shoulders
taking hearts
to convert hostage

But I owe you the whole story
from the first syllable of dawn
until the center of this violent spiral
that is calling to us

history had launched into its mad dash
and as with a child's game
good and evil were schoolmates
playing hide-and-seek playing hopscotch
practicing with the words and weapons of the strong
in a peaceful barnyard
where laughter was discouraged

Then there were trip wires
conspiracies hatched in the shadows
anonymously crafted plans
secrets shuttled
to couriers at the gates of the Palace
where the Enchanter with great pomp raised his voice
and things fell into a trance

The humans followed the voice of God on Earth
they never lost the trail
they dressed virtuously
and worshipped banknotes
whose perfumes they tracked

VIII

Yes this country nicknamed miracle
ignored the blood spilled
promised to inoculate the wind
with shots of peace

inconvenient flare-ups
and any hints of resistance
were snuffed in the womb
with the spook of a moonbeam

prisons and barbed wire flourished
in the shadow of the foothills
and large trees

And so the corrective rays spread
pressing his vision

into the cycle of days and suns
the hoarse voice of the Enchanter
fit the pieces of moon back together set a wreath
on the heads of the wise and of the terrible children

IX

There were speeches and rivers
to swim across
the ancestors were subjected to mysterious trials
but the ancestors no longer spoke
ancient voices buried away from the city
they regarded nothing but the distant shadows
silhouettes floating on heat-baked roads
the power tended to its business
sorted grains for the people by name
fed those faithful to the court

the humans deprived of myths assimilated
those murderish words architectures of nothingness

In the middle of the day the surprise
passed through secret pathways
the divine words nourished
the homeless
lifted up spirits
lost in illusion

it was Christmas at the end of the century
the surprise flaunted its wings
under the windows
in the city streets
before the huts
across the open countryside
the surprise reflected the emaciated faces
of the terrible children dressed in camouflage
waving machine guns

a hail of bullets flooded the country
swept the Palace which fell backward on itself

The market exploded with pent-up joy
and the surprise gleefully overflowed
from a vase of fear that had been kept sealed since the beginning

Christmas was born in the crowd
and the crowd divvied itself in communion
hoping to greet time
which walked
finally in jubilant spirals of optimism

under the midday sun the crowd wrote
its dreams for the future's appointment with the dawn

X

Tell me how to spread seed
for such wild dreams
when the forces of darkness
inhabit the *uniformed body*
just so they can break the wings of the wind

tell me that the sun was too beautiful
for a Christmas like all the others

the century was not yet finished
and the future had stopped breathing

The day's prayer makes its appeal
a baleful litany reeking of indecent plots
as if Africa could not imagine
a scapegoat more capable of holding
the popular imagination hostage

today the sky stays low
the word is ready to laugh
its new syllables endorse
any new color of the season

Yesterday was a *black cat*
today a *white knight*
then a *black Mercedes*
with that first stone Evil inaugurates
its underground kingdom
between the white and the black
only the soil where man hunts man
discharges the scent of the red carpet

Yet we've sung in chorus
hope-artist whose hands are in the rainbow

when riding this fever of the manhunt
the past is shortsighted
and the future dreams of twilight's tests

The chagrined spirits lift off
in swarms of bees
dressed in letters and numbers crippled
crumpled bruised or whole

here we shed the prison years
the mental torture endured
between such honeyed walls of refuge
today all the letters of nobility
gather out in the broad daylight
we plow the Edenic garden
plant flower after flower
on the new blood-colored ground

XI

There are thick heads
slumbering in the aisles of power
subscribing to an edition of history
that traces its circle
around the same umbilicus
as if no one
but the tenants of the Palace
could ever be born in the sun's gaze

They told the tales of people
innocent in all ways
who at first light would be allowed
to prop the palm fronds over hope

here laziness assumes itself as the law
lounging in office hammocks
sprawled in waiting rooms
there where work once inspired the Law

Into what shallow depths
have we fallen
which hell do we cross from dawn to noon
and in which abandoned dumpsters
the values
formerly declared of public interest

The new messiahs network across
the Dalmatian map
to chew artlessly on
the world's connective tissue while we watch
their weapon a stiff blank speech
that hacks the timeless culture
into morsels
pulverized stones and flint crumbs
ignite the lines that weave a life of sharp contrast

My God deliver us from hyenas
from the tawny heads of these dream vandals
because education is not a trap
invented by pilgrims who arrive
to shatter the foundations
I'm sure now that it braids
the grandeur of the soul to the aureole of sincerity
the foundational coupling that unites us
around the source of Kindness

How do I tell you that the day
falls
in the scree of teardrop rain
because the writ issued
from the peaks of power
lacks terms of reconciliation

tomorrow the future has an appointment with the dawn
and I do not know what enfant terrible
startled by the aurora's clarity
will take the chance to throw that first stone
across the moat that circumscribes power

A MURDERED LIFE

I

Born at the edge of the clouds
the raindrops
braided you out of vines in the cradle
the djinnis had accompanied you
to the tree kingdom
and among the green leaves
you had heard

it will bring silence
to the village of men

The mother welcomed the child
like an esteemed guest
the child's heritage included
three drops of lemon
under the tongue
to light the voice's path

do not lose your grip at the doors of silence
because your words will not fall from the sky
they are grains of sand
flavored with salt and that interminably hot pepper

In the hands of the painter
the aurora exhausted its miraculous palette
illuminated a break in the clouds
you had opened your eyes
deep in the wonders of nature
your skin learned the hard laws
of human life

The tales of life
were neither beautiful nor happy
winding from toil to toil
footpaths of courage odor of tenacity
tales of the transient life
that added
days to the hours of each
day mingled with your skin
with the sun's rays
the light of new hands

II

Moons radiant beads
to tally
the time lived in the glint of your eye
you invented that chiaroscuro spark
of ordinary life
traveled by moon and by sun
you dressed yourself in permanence
the sun kept you company
as you traveled to the country of the young man
in whose skin
you built your dwelling

The dreams hastening off
toward those banks of hope
this child's tale
in the right hand
on sheets of papyrus curled
into smiles by the early winds
the dawn was slow to assign
the day's course
you young man you pursued
the rhythms of your life
for tomorrow
for all eternity

your blood and your veins
beat drums
at the shutters of your heart
which fanned a flame in your body

Eyes open
to the fragile extremities of time
on the ground of suffering
in the hunger lining the sidewalks
the asphalt of miserable streets
saved now by water in the city
you smiled at any wind
once the word
unraveled the syllables of this world

Your head bobbed in the musical sea
navigated there in the waves
and rhythms of tomorrow
the lines of your left hand
concealed the secrets of departure
to decrypt to understand
from aurora to twilight

the nights to come populate your dreams
unaware of the labyrinth's meaning
did you know
what forest you would cross
what mountain crease would deliver you
to that threshold of departure

III

Young man of the seas and sands
lost in life's haze
walking with eyes wide despite the brightness
but in the shade of the eternal
choice has lost track of your steps
time's key has been swiped

in the lines of your left hand
the blood of fear
bespeaks
your life's brevity

And the signs of the coming rupture
tiptoe across your lips
your bursts of laughter kindle kindness
the complexion of your soul
tints the transparent light
balances the resistance of the sky
opens doors behind which words of happiness
have been hoarded
a strongbox in the corner of the heart
and the day husks these remarks
like an ancestor in the shade of a ficus
who has gone astray in the streets of the city

IV

Poet to your hours
foreign to those of your moment
with whom you've bonded
surviving the streets
you innovate games
dredge them from the mud of time
you fish the roses of sand
to hand-polish
to open like fresh oysters
to present at the sun's high point
to wash the rare pearls in the water of Kindness

Near the door of those who know everything
you pass your mind says filthy
those who know everything
wear the skin of God on Earth
live atop the mountains
of money deal in immediate gains
they ignore the ordeal of meeting
thread to the needle that stitches dreams
young man left for dead
you sing the hope of direct speech
unseen iconoclast
in the garden of new monuments
guarded night and day by machine guns

There are no friends on this Earth
but you shed light
at every street corner
while the world papers its walls
in new words
and you do not know yet
you who provide your smile immediately
to the sun
which told you on this afternoon
that you were wrong

V

Midday tapped its hours
and the city lurched into motion
hidden in the shadows
through the exchanges of suns and moons
you had passed the tests of otherness
defended by the double-edged sword of words
that shames you
marking your brow with scandal

now you know you wear a name
like no one else
a name that atones for an original sin
for the entire region

singular young man
cut from the common stone
you no longer have the right to speak nor a path forward
you are a third party you are it then

Out in the open a man in uniform
clubbed you
in compliance
you split at the temple like ripe fruit
you fell backward
he robbed you of loose change
the fruit of your night hour labors
and shredded your identity card
offered it
sprinkling a path for the moths

Generous soul providential guide
ordinary citizen doing his best
to safeguard the peace
an anonymous passer-by had shown to your house

the hyena-men
who convened between two ditches

you were not yet a dead man
under the sun of the ephemeral season
you had been provided the most direct route
and your life waited at the precipice of that forthcoming march

VI

You breathed the air of the country given to you
on that first morning of the world
first citrusy word under the tongue
first rain obstinacy of the streets

you no longer tasted freshness in the air
the scents from the wind conveyed
the fragrance of charred houses
and their flames ran on you
like utter comprehension across the skin

Because a wheel in flames
is the perfect burial plot
in the eyes of those who make the law
by wielding weapons
in peacetime

and orders are received to pacify the country
and the calm of the streets reflects
the lithic calm of cemeteries
o time suspend your flight
in the interval between time and eternity

the flames train those who remain sincere
in the elocution of the sacred gesture
to purify the earth

VII

A good soul guardian of the territory
had led the hyena-uniform
toward the district of strange men
they say
women who increase life
right in front of our eyes
children who roam in the streets
the neighborhood of the subhuman they say
came from elsewhere came from afar
and naturalize like moths
near trash heaps and gutters

VIII

The father recounted the order
injury in the side by firearm
the father pummeled
with igneous words the father beaten
the father ripped from side to side
the father heard the voice of the uniform in concert with the civilian
    voice
between two rivers of anger
he felt the tenuous thread of his son's life

the father hoarding the crumbs of their time together eyelids closed
between the swales of death and rivers of life
the father caught the murmuring of the hyena-man
made out
finish him beyond that trash with your machete
out of my view
from the muffled hyena voice

The father already dead in his skin
dead man whose dignity is trampled
by the keepers of the peace assassinated in the middle of the day
in that hatred cast by the keepers of the peace
the peace cremated everything afloat in that air of time

the father dead
a thousand times dead

IX

But the human garbage resurrected
rhizome or vermin squirreling along the ground
resistant tenacious
the human garbage multiplied itself
carried courage's flame
there amid the faces of the memorial to
the unspeakable

the faces
which no longer breathed

X

How to imagine the perfect word
when the sequence murders life at its source
when the baton crushes
human dignity
destroys *Liberty Leading the People*

on the path leading from Scio to Guernica
there is the new Rwandan monster
that multiplies at will
there is Côte d'Ivoire ablaze
with duplicitous speech

How to speak the beauty of the world
when life's hope
crumbles like yarrow

when death no longer presents an odor
of transformation in the fertile loam
where power blooms

ACKNOWLEDGMENTS

Excerpts from this collection originally appeared in *Seedings*, FUSION, the *North American Review,* the NEA Writer's Corner, and *EuropeNow*.

This project is supported in part by an award from the National Endowment for the Arts.

27 The Enchanter refers to Félix Houphouët-Boigny, the first president of Côte d'Ivoire (the Ivory Coast). Houphouët-Boigny was in office from the country's independence from French colonial rule in 1960 until his death in 1993.

32 The "surprise" refers to the Christmas coup d'état that removed Houphouët-Boigny's successor, Henri Konan Bedié, from power. Bedié was president from 1993 to 1999. Section two of the book, "A murdered life," recounts the killing of a young man during ethnic and political violence that followed in the Ivory Coast in 2000.

64 *o time suspend your flight* (*ô temps suspens ton vol*) is a quote from the poem "Le Lac" by Alphonse de Lamartine.

69 *Liberty Leading the People* refers to the painting by Eugène Delacroix that memorialized the July Revolution of 1830, also known as the "Three Glorious Days," which overthrew Charles X, the last Bourbon king of France.

69 Scio, or Chios, refers to the island that suffered a brutal reprisal by the Ottomans during the Greek war for independence in 1822. Eugène Delacroix's painting, *The Massacre at Chios*, portrays the destruction with little hope.

69 Guernica is a town in the Basque territory of Spain that was used for bombing practice by Nazi Germany. Francisco Franco's nationalist Spanish government requested the bombardment, which did not distinguish between military and civilian targets. Pablo Picasso responded to the event with his 1937 mural titled *Guernica*.

*Eight New-Generation African
Poets: A Chapbook Box Set*
Edited by Kwame Dawes
and Chris Abani
(Akashic Books)

*New-Generation African Poets:
A Chapbook Box Set (Nne)*
Edited by Kwame Dawes
and Chris Abani
(Akashic Books)

*New-Generation African Poets:
A Chapbook Box Set (Tatu)*
Edited by Kwame Dawes
and Chris Abani
(Akashic Books)

*New-Generation African Poets:
A Chapbook Box Set (Tano)*
Edited by Kwame Dawes
and Chris Abani
(Akashic Books)

To order or obtain more information on these or other University of
Nebraska Press titles, visit nebraskapress.unl.edu. For more information
about the African Poetry Book Series, visit africanpoetrybf.unl.edu.